WOMEN *in* MUSIC

Aaaaa Piigh

'There is no sex in art.'
ETHEL SMYTH

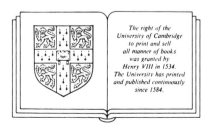

The right of the
University of Cambridge
to print and sell
all manner of books
was granted by
Henry VIII in 1534.
The University has printed
and published continuously
since 1584.

CAMBRIDGE UNIVERSITY PRESS

Cambridge   New York   Port Chester   Melbourne   Sydney

Published by the Press Syndicate of the University of Cambridge
The Pitt Building, Trumpington Street, Cambridge CB2 1RP
40 West 20th Street, New York, NY 10011-4211, USA
10 Stamford Road, Oakleigh, Melbourne 3166, Australia

First published 1991

Printed in Great Britain by Scotprint Limited, Musselburgh

A catalogue record for this book is available from the British Library.

ISBN 0 521 34677 0

Acknowledgements

The author and publishers would like to thank the following for permission to reproduce copyright material.

Photographs
Title page Format photographs Ltd (Val Wilmer); pp. 4, 14, Bodleian Library, University of Oxford (p. 4: MS.Don a.3, fol.85; p. 14: MS.Rawl.liturg.e.36, fol.90v.); p. 5 (top left) and p. 60, Hanya Chlala; p. 5 (top centre) and p. 55, David Lumsdaine; p. 5 (top right) and p. 51, Suzie E. Maeder; p. 5 (bottom), Stuart Hastain; p. 6: top left, Jean-Pierre Leloir; top right, Chi-Chi Nwanoku; bottom left, Brian Harrison; bottom right, Walter Schels; p. 7, John Wright; pp. 8, 17 and 32, Mary Evans Picture Library; p. 10, by permission of the British Library (Cotton.Dom.A.XVII.f.177v); p. 12, Pinacoteca of Querini Stampalia Foundation, Venice; p. 20, National Archives of Canada; p. 22, Associated Press, New York; p. 23, Clive Barda; p. 24, Sarah Ainslie; p. 25, Hulton Picture Co.; p. 26, Val Wilmer; pp. 27, 29, 30, Redferns; p. 37, Rheinisches Bildarchiv, Stadt Köln; p. 43, Staatliche Kunstsammlungen Dresden; p. 44, Performing Arts Research Center, New York Public Library; p. 47: top left, National Portrait Gallery; bottom right, The Archives, The Royal Opera House.

Passages on p. 13 from Vol.1 of *Dr Burney's Musical Tours in Europe*, edited by Percy A. Scholes, Oxford University Press, 1959, reproduced by permission of Oxford University Press.

Music
p. 11, extract from fifteenth-century hymnal from Barking Abbey: Master and Fellows of Trinity College, Cambridge.
p. 35, 'Reap the Flax': © 1989 Silver Burdett & Ginn. Used with permission. All rights reserved.
p. 38 Hildegard of Bingen 'O Ignis Spiritus': reproduced by permission of Antico Edition.
pp. 40–41, 'Aure Volante' by Caccini: © The Trustees of The Smith College 1945.
p. 46 Clara Schumann 'Andante con Sentimento': © 1979 by Ludwig Doblinger (Bernhard Herzmansky) KG, Wien, München, edited by Rosario Marciano, reproduced by permission of Aldred A. Kalmus Ltd.
pp. 53–54 Thea Musgrave 'Rorate Coeli', pp. 56–7 Nicola LeFanu 'The Same Day Dawns', and pp. 58–59 Nicola LeFanu 'Chiaroscuro': all reproduced by permission of Novello & Co. Ltd.

Every effort has been made to reach copyright holders; the publishers would be glad to hear from anyone whose rights they have unknowingly infringed.

Title page photograph:
Annie Whitehead, the rock, pop and jazz trombonist who played with the Ivy Benson All-Girl Dance Band before setting up her own quintet. She is a member of several Latin and jazz bands and regularly plays guest sessions.

Cover illustration: *Sue Hillwood-Harris*

GO

CONTENTS

'SO, NAME A WOMAN COMPOSER, THEN!'

More young people than ever before are playing in school or county orchestras, brass or jazz bands and in pop and rock groups. Perhaps you or your friends do. If so, next time you are at a concert, whether you are playing or singing, or whether you are in the audience, try this experiment. Count how many boys and how many girls are performing, and notice which instruments they are playing. The chances are that you will find the sexes equally represented and playing the full range of instruments.

These days people are less surprised to see girls playing saxophones or drums, and it is not unusual to find all-girl groups dominating the pop charts. But it has not always been like this. Even now there are still more men than women in our major symphony orchestras, and women conductors are still few and far between. Why is this? There is no simple answer. But it certainly has nothing to do with women being less musical than men.

Women have always made music but not always the same kind of music as men, often because their lifestyles have been different. Until fairly recently women never played trumpets and drums because these were instruments associated with war, in which women did not take part. A less satisfactory reason was that women were thought to be too weak to play these instruments.

In some religions women have not taken part in music during the various ceremonies. You still find this in some Christian denominations today. If you go to an Anglican cathedral, for example, you are not likely to find women or girls in the choir, although the situation is gradually changing. But in other religions and at other times women have made a very important contribution to the music during worship. Egyptian tomb paintings and vases from Ancient Greece often show priestesses playing musical instruments.

Until recently, women were expected to confine themselves to creating a home for their husbands and children. So it is not surprising that a lot of music made by women has been of the type that could be played at home: solo songs and chamber

A female harpist entertaining at court. From a French manuscript of the early sixteenth century.

Who are these twentieth-century composers?
(Answers at the bottom of this page.)

music, for example. Since there is a limit to the amount of sound you can listen to in a confined space, this music was naturally played on quiet instruments, like the lute, harp or piano. In the past, the ability to play instruments like these and to sing were thought to be accomplishments that all girls should have, so that they could entertain guests at home. But any girl wanting to play a wider range of instruments or to follow a professional career in music and play or sing in public (or publish her compositions) usually met with prejudice and discouragement.

Composers tend to write music for instruments with which they are familiar. Little wonder then that women have not composed for full orchestras as men have. This is why it is hard to think of a female composer who is as well-known as Mozart or Beethoven. Another reason is that, for a long time, women were not given the chance to learn how to compose. But now that more and more opportunities are open to women, composers like Phyllis Tate, Judith Weir, Thea Musgrave and Nicola LeFanu are writing music that is performed regularly.

In pop music too there has been a big change in the role of women over the last thirty years. Women singers have always been popular, but now all-female groups like the Bangles are reaching the charts, and there are more women instrumentalists. Women are also breaking into management, production, journalism, publicity and publishing in the field of music.

Today women are actively involved in every branch of the pop and classical scenes, doing exactly the same kinds of jobs as men. They have had to work hard to get there, although no doubt it helps that it is now generally more acceptable for women to have a career as well as a family. In this book, you can read about the musical achievements of women both now and in the past. You may well find that there are more 'women in music' than you think.

Claire Briggs, Principal Horn-player with the City of Birmingham Symphony Orchestra.

From left to right: Judith Weir, Nicola LeFanu and Elizabeth Maconchy.

5

WOMEN *as* PERFORMERS

'Home is where the harp is'

At the end of one gig, Annie Whitehead, the rock, pop and jazz trombonist, was told that it was a pity that she played the trombone because it hid her face.

This is not very different from the opinion of one American conductor in 1904:

Nature never intended the fair sex to become cornettists, trombonists and players of wind instruments. In the first place, they are not strong enough to play them as well as men . . . Another point against them is that women cannot play brass instruments and look pretty and why should they spoil their good looks?

Compare this with what the Italian nobleman Castiglione had to say in 1528:

Imagine what an ungainly sight it would be to have a woman playing drums, fifes, trumpets and other instruments of that sort.

Five outstanding contemporary female performers: the pianist Mitsuko Uchida (top left), the double bass player Chi-Chi Nwanoku (top right), the violinist Kyung Wha Chung (bottom left), the pianist Kathryn Stott (bottom right), and the 'cellist Ofra Harnoy (this page).

The harpsichord was considered ideal for eighteenth-century women. A quiet instrument, not needing accompaniment, it could be played in the privacy of the home and did not spoil the player's looks.

A suitable instrument for a woman

For hundreds of years, women have been discouraged from playing certain instruments because they were thought to be too weak to do so, or because they would spoil their appearance in the process. The argument has been used not only against drums, wind and brass but also against many other instruments such as the bass guitar. For example, before the nineteenth century, women were not considered strong enough to play the viola, and the BBC was still banning women 'cellists from its orchestras in the 1930s. According to the composer Ethel Smyth, this was because it was felt that the way a 'cellist sat was 'an unseemly one for women'.

So what kinds of instruments *have* women been encouraged to play? In the past, a musically accomplished woman would play instruments like the harp, guitar and various kinds of keyboard – the spinet, harpsichord and, more recently, the piano. What these instruments have in common is that you can play both tunes and chords on them, which means that they can be played by one person without any accompaniment. (This is unlike the trumpet, for example, where you need a piano or a whole band of other instruments to give it its full effect.) They are also quiet enough to be played indoors and, if you want to, you can sing whilst you are playing them.

In other words, they are ideal instruments for a woman spending her life at home, making music for her own amusement or for the entertainment of her family and friends. Of course, the home was where women were expected to be and, no doubt, many women were happy with this and enjoyed the music they made there. But the problem came whenever they wanted to branch out and become professional musicians. There was little chance of women joining bands and orchestras, because they did not play the right kinds of instrument. Women were often poorly trained, even on the instruments thought to be 'suitable' for them. And there was a general feeling that it was 'not proper' for women to perform in public.

It was very much the same with singing. Women sang in the privacy of their own homes. But they were not trained or encouraged to sing in public and it was a long time before they were allowed to sing the liturgy in church services or to sing on the stage.

There were exceptions, however, as you will see when you read on.

This is how Annie Whitehead describes her early musical experiences:
I wanted to play tuba at first, but they wouldn't let me. They didn't say it's because I was a girl, they said, 'You couldn't possibly play a tuba, it's much too big and you're much too small.'

1 Do you feel that you have ever been discouraged from playing a particular instrument, just because of your sex? If so, which instrument was it?
  - Ask your friends, family and teachers the same question and keep a record of their answers.
  - Look at those answers carefully.

2 Are there any instruments which are particularly associated with either men or women? Think, for example, of the harp, the trumpet, and the saxophone.
  - Is there any difference between the instruments which men and women have been discouraged from learning?
  - Can you draw any conclusions from all this?

Convent music-making

From the earliest times, much the best way of getting a good musical training if you were a woman was to become a nun. As a nun you would learn to read music in order to sing the various services which were such an important part of the daily life of the convent.

By the sixteenth and seventeenth centuries, many convents had become famous throughout Europe for their music-making. A newspaper of 1678 describes the abbey of Longchamps, France, as having such wonderful music 'that nothing so beautiful is to be heard in any other convent'. But it was probably in Italy that convent music-making reached its peak, especially in the cities of Milan and Ferrara.

These medieval nuns would have had far more opportunities for music-making than other women of the time.

We know that Milan had at least five very famous musical convents at this time. In 1670, the nuns at one of these – the convent of Santa Radegonda – were described as 'the first singers in Italy', a reputation which they kept for many years. Several of the nuns at Milan became well-known soloists. At the convent of Maria Annunciata, for example, Claudia Sessa drew such huge crowds to hear her that, during important services, most of the congregation had to stand outside.

It was not just their singing that made these nuns famous. Most convents had large orchestras, and the nuns played a wide range of instruments, not just the few that were thought to be suitable for women. For instance, in the 1590s the convent of San Vito in Ferrara had an orchestra which boasted cornetti, trombones, violins, viole bastarde, double harps, cornamuses (variations of the bagpipes) and harpsichords. This showed quite clearly that it was absurd to think that women could not play wind and brass instruments. In fact, one writer of the time tells us that the nuns at San Vito played the cornetti and trombones 'with such grace, and with such a nice manner and with such sonorous and just intonation of notes that even people who are esteemed most excellent in the profession confess that it is incredible to anyone who does not see and hear it'.

The 'concerto di donne'

Around the same time, Ferrara was the scene of another very important event in women's musical history. In 1580, Alfonso d'Este, the Duke of Ferrara, hired three 'ladies-in-waiting'. Not unusual, except that this title was a disguise. These women had really been brought to court because of their beautiful voices, and they were now to be paid to sing at the private concerts which the Duke put on for his own entertainment and that of friends and family. It had always been perfectly acceptable for women at court to make music, but it was most 'unladylike' to be paid for doing so. So it was to protect the women's reputation that such elaborate measures were

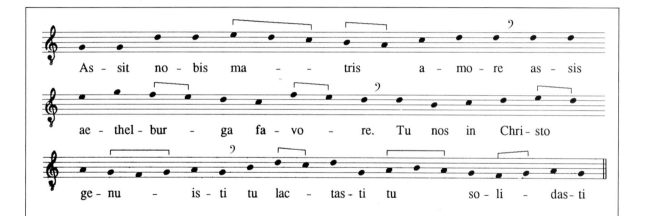

As - sit no - bis ma - - tris a - mo - re as - sis

ae - thel - bur - ga fa - vo - re. Tu nos in Chri - sto

ge - nu - is - ti tu lac - tas - ti tu so - li - das - ti

An extract from a fifteenth-century hymnal from Barking Abbey which contains the text and music of three hymns in honour of St Ethelburga, the first abbess of Barking in the seventh century. There is no indication of the author, but this is likely to be a woman as the manuscript originated in a convent.

Try singing this alone, or in a group. Remember to keep the sound flowing, and take a breath where ⌐ is indicated above the music. Before doing this, listen to recordings of plain chant to get an idea of the style.

taken to hide the real reason for their being at court.

Alfonso was very proud of his women singers and used them to impress his friends. Not that he was always successful. When the old Duke of Mantua heard them, he stormed out of the concert shouting, 'I would rather be an ass than a lady'. But their fame soon spread and before long the idea was being copied by the other rulers in northern Italy and southern Germany. There was a group of women musicians at the court of Duke Fernando di Medici in Florence as early as 1584 and even in Mantua by 1587. In fact, by 1600, there was hardly a court without its female group or *concerto di donne*. By that time, the idea had become so respectable that there was no need to hide what such women's work really was.

The first professional musicians

The women were hired for their voices above all, although they would have accompanied themselves on the viol and harp. Some, however, also became famous instrumentalists like the two cornett players in Mantua and the viola bastarda

player in the *concerto* of Lucrezia d'Este, a leading Italian noblewoman.

So brilliant was one woman harpist in a particular Roman household that a certain Cardinal Montalto vowed to go on a fast just to hear her play.

But whether they were singers, instrumentalists or both does not really matter. The important point is that, in the closing years of the sixteenth century, women had the chance, for the first time, to carve careers for themselves as professional musicians.

Although the courts of the nobility were the main source of employment, quite a few women also performed at meetings of musical and literary societies held at the houses of wealthy intellectuals. This was certainly the case in Venice which was a republic at the time and therefore did not have a royal court.

Other very important centres for female musicians in Venice were the *ospedali* or *conservatori*.

Women in the conservatoires of the seventeenth and eighteenth centuries

Anyone training at a college of music today will study several subjects, including composition, music history, acoustics and electronics, as well as learning to play one or more instruments to the highest professional standard. Schools offering this kind of training were first established in Italy, probably the most famous being the one at Naples, founded in 1537. Unfortunately these schools only accepted boys.

In the seventeenth century, however, several similar schools were set up in Venice, this time for girls. Known as *ospedali* or hospitals, they were originally meant to give orphaned and destitute girls a free education and to prepare them for a trade. But they soon became so famous that they began to attract fee-paying pupils from all over Europe.

The four best-known *ospedali* were I Mendicanti, La Pietà, L'Incurabili and Gli Derelitti. There, girls were trained to sing and to play a wide range of instruments. They were also given a tremendous amount of performance experience, and the chance to play in orchestras. At first, they played only in the chapels of their own *ospedali* or at private parties in the houses of noble families. But by the eighteenth century they were giving large-scale, public concerts, often as state occasions in honour of distinguished visitors to Venice.

An all-women orchestra from one of Venice's conservatoires performing at a concert in 1782. From a painting by Gabriele Bella.

'No instrument is large enough to frighten them'

Among these distinguished visitors was a certain Charles de Brosses, the President of the Parliament of Burgundy, who visited Italy in the years 1739–40. In a letter, he describes how the girls at the *ospedali*:

sing like angels, play the viola, flute, organ, oboe, cello, bassoon – in short, no instrument is large enough to frighten them . . . The performances are entirely their own, and each concert is composed of about forty young women.

It was not just the range of instruments which impressed de Brosses, but also the way they were played. 'Of the four orphanages,' he writes, 'I go most to the Ospedali della Pietà. It ranks first for the perfection of its symphonies.' He argues that this is better even than the orchestra of the Paris Opéra – which, at that time, was widely regarded as the best in Europe.

Another distinguished visitor to the Venetian *ospedali* was the English musician Dr Charles Burney. In his diary entry for 17th August 1771, he gives an account of a two-hour concert which he has just heard in I Mendicanti:

. . . it was really curious to see, as well as to hear, every part of this concert, performed by female violins, hautbois, tenors, bases, harpsichords, French horns and even double bases.

'The singing', he tells us, was also 'really excellent in different styles.' Not everybody was enthusiastic, however. The famous Englishwoman Mrs Hester Thrale, describing her visit in 1789, complains that

the sight of girls . . . handling the double bass, and blowing into the bassoon did not much please me.

Many of the women from *ospedali* were also fine soloists whose fame spread far beyond Italy. As Dr Burney again tells us, it was at I Mendicanti that

two celebrated female performers . . . Signora Guglielmi, and Signora Maddalena Lombardini-Sirmen, who have received such great and just applause in England, had their musical instruction.

Guglielmi was a singer, while Lombardini-Sirmen was a violinist and composer.

---

1 Go to the music section of your school or local library and look for pictures of a cornett, a viola bastarda, a double harp, a cornamuse and a harpsichord.

If there are none in the books in stock, ask the librarian to recommend other possible sources. For example, several museums have collections of ancient instruments. They might be able to help you by sending you copies of their catalogue.

2 Try to hear recordings of these types of instruments. Here again your music librarian should be able to help by suggesting records, tapes or CDs you could borrow. There is also a *Listening list* on pages 63–64 of this book. Sometimes you can hear recordings on the radio or on television.

Women in the conservatoires and music schools of the nineteenth and twentieth centuries

So impressed was Dr Burney by what he had heard and seen in Venice that, as soon as he got back to England, he tried to set up a conservatoire of his own. His own 'Plan for a Music School' never got off the ground, but others were more successful. In the late eighteenth and early nineteenth centuries, conservatoires began to spring up all over Europe, in cities like Prague, Vienna, Leipzig and Paris. The first British conservatoire was the Royal Academy of Music which was set up in 1822 and given a royal charter in 1839. Right from the start it took as many women students as men. This was very important because, at the time, women had no hope of getting into universities to study music – or any other subject for that matter.

Australia and the United States soon followed, with conservatoires being set up in Adelaide, Melbourne, Ohio, Chicago, New York and Boston. One of the teachers at the Boston Conservatory of Music was Julius Eichberg who won quite a reputation for insisting on teaching the violin to women as well as to men. Indeed, he went further, writing in one magazine in 1879 that 'we gladly espouse the cause of women's rights to play upon all the instruments of the orchestra'.

To prove the point, he formed his students into the 'Eichberg Ladies' String Quartet' and the 'Eichberg String Orchestra'. He must have been very successful in breaking down the old prejudices because by 1888, the *Boston Herald* was reporting that 'the girl of today will astonish no one, even if she carries about the cornet or trombone, as well as the violin'.

The Holywell Music Room, Oxford, the first concert hall in Europe, opened in 1748. It is still regularly used for recitals.

Women solo concert artists

So, during the eighteenth and nineteenth centuries, it gradually became possible for women to get more or less the same standard of professional musical training, on as wide a range of instruments, as men. But it is one thing to be trained, and another to get a job which makes use of that training.

Here, women performers were helped by another important change. Before the eighteenth century, nearly all professional music-making took place in churches (where it formed part of worship), in the theatre, or as a private entertainment in the houses of the nobility. All these institutions had their own permanent musicians who were paid to work there and nowhere else.

But then, during the eighteenth century, there was a gradual move towards public music concerts, rather like those you can hear today. Concert halls were built and musicians were hired for a particular concert and paid out of ticket proceeds, instead of being employed on a permanent basis. This meant that performers – especially soloists – had far more freedom to come and go as they chose and to play when and where they wanted. The popularity of the new concerts also meant that there was far more work available than ever before.

A new breed of soloists such as the violinist Niccolò Paganini and the pianist Franz Liszt began touring from city to city and country to country, attracting the kind of publicity and building up the following that today we associate with pop stars. Now that they were able to get the right kind of training, women soloists soon began to join their ranks.

One of the earliest of these was Maria Theresia von Paradis, a blind pianist and composer who, in the years 1784 to 1786, toured Europe playing in Paris, London, Berlin, Prague and a number of other cities. Critics of the time praised her faultless, precise and polished performances. She was followed by such personalities as the American pianist Amy Fay (1844–1928) and Camilla Urso (1842–1902). Urso was the first woman ever to study the violin at the Paris Conservatoire and, according to her own account, 'the first girl violinist heard in the United States'. She performed widely in Europe, the United States, Canada and Australia.

1 Find out where the nearest music college to your home is, and write for a syllabus to see what subjects students follow there.

2 Find out whether men and women study all instruments in equal numbers there.
   Before doing so, discuss with your class and teacher:
   - how to go about collecting the information without causing too much inconvenience to the music school and yourselves
   - how best to present the information so that the results are clear.

3 Try to listen to some recordings of music by composers such as Liszt.

Clara Schumann (1819–96)

By far the most famous woman performer of the nineteenth century was the pianist Clara (pronounced *Klaara*) Schumann. The eldest child of Friedrick and Marianne Wieck, she was born in Leipzig, Germany, on 13th September 1819. Even before her birth, her father had decided that she was to be a brilliant pianist. When she was five, he began to give her piano lessons and to take her to concerts and the opera. She also studied music theory, singing and composition and learnt French and English, ready for her tours abroad.

As a very small child, she gave several piano recitals at home for her father's friends and she was still only nine when she made her first public appearance. Three years later, in 1831, she went on her first tour, travelling as far as Paris. By the age of sixteen she was famous throughout Europe.

Early tours

Her most successful tour in these early years was the one she made to Vienna in 1837. There she was greeted with the enthusiasm only ever accorded to the very greatest soloists. Her concerts were all sold out and she played to wild applause and brilliant reviews. One critic wrote:

The appearance of this artist can be regarded as epoch-making, for the highest level of artistic skill combined with the greatest genius, as was the case here, is only rarely to be found.

When Franz Liszt, probably the greatest pianist of the day, heard her, he wrote to the press in France and Germany, enthusing about her 'complete technical mastery, depth and sincerity of feeling'.

The Viennese music publishers bombarded her with requests for compositions because they knew that anything by her was be sure to be a great commercial success. But she was so busy giving concerts and being entertained by the most important people in the city, that she only had two hours left each day to compose. Even so, she eventually became a very fine composer, as we shall see later.

During this and earlier tours, her father made all the arrangements. But in 1839 her father refused to accompany her on a concert tour to Paris. He was annoyed because she wanted to marry a man of whom he did not approve. He presumably hoped she would find it impossible to rent halls and instruments, hire supporting musicians, arrange publicity and cope with other practical aspects of her tour. In fact, Clara proved more than capable in these matters and the tour was another success. From then on she took charge of her own affairs.

A two-career marriage

In 1840, after taking her case to court (she was under age, and, as her father had refused permission, she had to get the court to over-ride his decision), she married the composer Robert Schumann. At first, they faced the same kinds of problems that modern couples face when both partners have careers. Robert wanted his wife to go on touring but was not ready to give up composing to help her. In the same way, Clara was a great supporter of her husband's work but worried that it was destroying her own career:

My piano playing is falling behind again. This always happens when Robert is composing. Not even one little hour in the day can be found for me. If only I don't fall too far behind.

They gradually managed to find a balance. In 1842, Clara was invited to play in Copenhagen. After a great deal of soul-searching she went, leaving Robert to look after their baby. While he was happy with this, many people found it very odd at the time.

Clara was not one to be held back by gossip. In those days, no woman would ever be seen in public in the last months of a pregnancy. Clara, however, gave concerts right up to the birth of several of her eight children.

When Robert died in 1856 after a long illness, he left Clara with a large family to support. Clara's answer was to throw herself even more wholeheartedly into her career.

In all, she gave over 1300 public concerts in England, Europe and Russia. She was also responsible for changing the whole pattern of piano recitals.

Clara Schumann, one of the foremost pianists and composers of the nineteenth century, pictured with her husband the composer Robert Schumann.

The art of the recital

In the nineteenth century, soloists usually played pieces which allowed them to show off to their audiences. Clara did not approve of this. She chose instead to play pieces which displayed the composer's talents, rather than her own. She gave the first public performances of many of the piano works of Beethoven, Chopin, Brahms and Robert Schumann. She was the first soloist ever to play from memory and one of the first to give a whole concert without any help from supporting artists.

No other nineteenth-century pianist – male or female – had as long nor as distinguished a career as Clara Schumann. Her sixtieth birthday was celebrated throughout the musical world. At this time she became principal piano teacher at the Frankfurt Conservatoire, and she trained many students from all over Europe and North and South America who came to study with her. She made her last public appearance in 1891 in Frankfurt, and it was there that she died, five years later.

---

1 **You have read about Clara Schumann. Now try to find the names of other female solo artists from the nineteenth and early twentieth centuries.**

2 **Keep a record, over a five- or six-week period, of all the solo concert artists you see live or on television. Note which instruments they play.**
   - **Are there some instruments which are more popular than others amongst women?**

3 **Name five female solo concert artists who are currently enjoying great popularity.**

4 **Find and listen to a recording by Clara Schumann. Some are given in the *Listening list*.**

Women in orchestras

Whether they are male or female, only those who reach the very highest performing standards can ever hope to earn a living as a soloist. Few reach that level, and so most trained musicians have to rely on orchestras, chamber groups, bands and so on for work. At first, this proved very difficult for women instrumentalists.

The problem was that most orchestras refused, on principle, to employ women. From about the 1850s, campaigns were launched all over England and the United States to try to change the situation. But as late as 1893, in a speech at the Chicago World Fair, Camillo Urso was still complaining about the 'many hundred good (women) violinists who are now without work' because of orchestral recruitment policies. Eventually it was decided that a better tactic would be for women performers to get together to set up their own orchestras. The idea started in Austria and Germany but soon spread to other parts of Europe.

The all-women orchestras

One of the first all-women orchestras was the Wiener Damen Orchester. The sensation created by its visit to New York in 1871 led immediately to similar groups being set up all over the United States. The New York Ladies' Elite was one of these. Most of the all-female orchestras played for concerts, private parties and in hotels and restaurants. They concentrated on arrangements of popular music-hall songs and light classical pieces. But for many audiences, the main attraction was not the music but the sight of a large number of women players gathered in one place. If a member of an orchestra became ill and no other woman player could be found, a man would be drafted in to play in drag!

Not all women musicians were happy to be treated like some kind of side-show or to be limited to one type of music. They wanted to play the full repertoire, including symphonies and concertos, to give large-scale concerts and to arrange concert tours just like any male orchestra.

This is exactly what the New York Women's String Orchestra and the Boston Fadette Lady Orchestra did. In all, this last orchestra gave over

6000 concerts and gained a nationwide reputation in the USA.

In 1903, American women musicians were allowed to join the Musical Union for the first time. Technically they could now become members of any orchestra. In fact, apart from harpists (who were seen to play a 'typically female' instrument), they still met with a lot of resistance, especially from male conductors. Here is a typical comment:

It would be like oil and water to put men and women in the same organization. Women musicians alone may be all right but they don't belong with men.

It was claimed both in Europe and the United States that women should be kept out of orchestras because they were quarrelsome, would not practise regularly, would turn up late and could not stand the long hours of rehearsals and performing. Such arguments did not pass unchallenged. For example, Ada Heinemann, a player in New York's Atlantic Garden Music Hall Orchestra, felt sure that:

A great many of us would hold our own with the majority of men. All we need is the chance.

In the early twentieth century, however, most job

Frau Amann-Weinlich conducting her Damenorchester. From an illustration in a Leipzig newspaper in 1873.

opportunities for women instrumentalists still came from the all-female orchestras. These were no longer confined to hotels and restaurants. The Depression of the 1930s meant that hotels, restaurants and resorts had to get rid of their orchestras, and the music theatres were forced to close down. Also, the talking movie had arrived, and cinemas no longer needed musicians.

Women began to set up full-scale symphony orchestras of eighty or more players. Among those founded in the 1920s, 1930s and 1940s were the Philadelphia Women's Symphony Orchestra, the American Women's Symphony Orchestra and the Women's Symphony Orchestra of Chicago. The last of these became so important that it had a regular series broadcasting throughout the United States.

'Mixed bathing in the sea of music'

This was still only a halfway house. What these women really wanted was to be members of mixed orchestras. There was a gradual move in that direction. In England, the conductor Sir Henry Wood made what has been called the first attempt at 'mixed bathing in the sea of music'. In the United States, the San Francisco Symphony Orchestra and the Pittsburg Symphony Orchestra began to admit women to their ranks.

The real change came with the Second World War (1939–45). Large numbers of male musicians were suddenly drafted into the forces and conductors were obliged to accept women in their place. When the war finished, most of these women kept their jobs. The mixed orchestra had at last arrived.

Not everyone was happy with this. Sir Thomas Beecham, a legendary conductor who was famous for his 'remarks', was all for dropping women from his orchestra after the war and, in 1959, he was still complaining that:

A pretty (woman) will distract the other musicians, and an ugly one will distract me.

The Ottawa Amateur Orchestral Society in 1898. This picture would seem to disprove the claim made by some writers of the time that men and women in an orchestra would be like oil and water, never mixing.

Even as recently as 1978, the conductor Zubin Mehta was reported to have said:

I just don't think women should be in an orchestra. They become men. Men treat them as equals . . .

Conductors are not always the ones who cause problems. When the clarinettist Sabine Meyer became the first woman player in the history of the Berlin Philharmonic Orchestra, most of the opposition came from fellow players. Because of the ill-feeling, she actually left the orchestra less than a year after her appointment. But most professional orchestras are now mixed, although a mixed orchestra with as many, or more women than men has still to be seen.

---

1 In 1938, a committee was set up in New York to find ways of combating 'unjust discrimination' against women orchestral players. One suggestion was that women should be given auditions for all orchestral jobs and that, during auditions, each player should be behind a screen.
  - **How effective do you think these measures would be?**
  - **Can you think of any other ways in which women could have been given a better chance of getting into an orchestra?**

2 **Find out how many women players, and how many men players, there are in famous orchestras like the London Symphony Orchestra, the BBC Symphony Orchestra, the Royal Philharmonic Orchestra, and the City of Birmingham Symphony Orchestra.**
  - **Why are there still, on average, more men than women in most orchestras?**

Women conductors

All-female orchestras, of course, also gave women the opportunity to follow careers as conductors. Caroline B. Nichols conducted the Boston Fadette Lady Orchestra between the years 1888 and 1920, while the Women's Symphony Orchestra of Chicago and the Boston Women's Symphony Orchestra had the good fortune to come under the baton of the English conductor and pianist Ethel Leginska. Leginska did not confine herself to all-female groups, but also conducted the New York Symphony Orchestra, the New York Philharmonic, and the Boston Philharmonic.

Antonia Brico (b. 1902)

Indeed, many women conductors, whilst supporting the cause of women instrumentalists, did not want to be confined to all-female orchestras, and felt that they needed to conduct major orchestras to establish their reputation. This was certainly true of the Dutch-born conductor Antonia Brico.

Brico studied in Germany. She created a sensation there in 1930 when she was the first woman to conduct the Berlin Philharmonic. She seemed set to become one of the leading conductors in Europe but, as a foreigner, she was obliged to leave Nazi Germany in 1932. She settled in the United States, but it was the height of the Depression and there was little work. Despite this, she managed to get some engagements and in 1934 formed the Women's Symphony Orchestra of New York.

Brico was against segregation of the sexes in music, however, and eventually reorganised the orchestra to include both men and women. Unfortunately it was the all-female aspect of the orchestra which had attracted audiences, and after a short time the group had to be disbanded. She also faced difficulties in her attempts to establish herself as a conductor of other mixed orchestras, as many people were still not comfortable with the idea of a woman conductor. One of her opponents was the rich arts patron Mrs Charles S. Guggenheimer, who effectively prevented her conducting the New York Philharmonic.

Antonia Brico, the first woman to conduct the Berlin Philharmonic Orchestra, conducting the Women's Symphony Orchestra of New York, which she founded in 1934.

Given the difficulties she faced, it is hardly surprising that Brico once said:

A woman must be five times better than a male if she is to succeed.

Indeed, the woman who had been set to become one of the leading conductors in Europe before the war had to content herself with spending many years as the conductor of the Denver Businessman's Orchestra. But in the late 1970s, with the appearance of a television documentary on her life, Brico was rediscovered and once again invited to conduct internationally famous orchestras. There can be no doubt that her work and experiences paved the way for many of the women conductors of the twentieth century.

Victoria Bond (b. 1950)

One of the leading American conductors of her generation, Victoria Bond was born in Los Angeles, and studied at the world-famous Juilliard School of Music under such eminent conductors as Pierre Boulez and Herbert von Karajan.

She is admired for her exciting technique, and has had conducting engagements with many orchestras including the Juilliard Orchestra, the Contemporary Music Ensemble, the New Amsterdam Symphony Orchestra and the Pittsburgh Symphony Orchestra. She has also guest conducted outside the United States.

She is a great champion of women composers, has written several articles about them and performed many of their works. In 1974 she was assistant conductor of a festival of women composers' works at Aptos, California. This included her own work *Suite aux Troubadours* which she not only conducted but also sang, displaying the great versatility and talent which is a mark of contemporary women musicians.

Jane Glover (b. 1949)

Since her professional debut at the Wexford Festival in 1975, Jane Glover has conducted some of the world's most famous orchestras, including the London Symphony Orchestra, the London Philharmonic Orchestra, the Royal Philharmonic Orchestra, the English Chamber Orchestra and the Netherlands Radio Chamber Orchestra. She has also become well known to the general public through her work as a documentary-maker and presenter on television.

She is an acknowledged expert on opera. It is not surprising to find that she has been musical director of the Glyndebourne Festival Opera and has appeared at Covent Garden.

Sian Edwards (b. 1959)

Although she was one of the first, Jane Glover was not *the* first woman conductor to appear at Covent Garden. That record is held by Sian Edwards, the winner of the Leeds Conductors' Competition in 1984, who conducted Michael Tippett's opera *The Knot Garden* there in 1988. She has also conducted performances with Scottish Opera and Glyndebourne Touring Opera, and has appeared at the Glyndebourne Festival. Her orchestral work has included engagements with the City of Birmingham Symphony

Jane Glover in rehearsal at Covent Garden.

Orchestra, the Royal Philharmonic Orchestra, the London Sinfonietta, the Orchestre de Paris and the San Francisco Symphony Orchestra.

Odaline de la Martinez (b. 1949)

Odaline de la Martinez, a Cuban by birth, now works in London where she is the founder of Lontano, a group which is primarily concerned with performing contemporary music, including electronic and computer-aided music, in which Martinez is particularly interested.

As well as conducting, she has composed a considerable amount of music which has been broadcast in several countries including Britain, Turkey, Ireland, Yugoslavia and the United States.

In an interview in *Musician* (the journal of the Musicians Union, December 1988) she underlines the crucial role of women conductors in changing attitudes:

If it is a sad, but chastening fact, as a recent LPO marketing report suggests, that the typical audience

Odaline de la Martinez, the Cuban-born conductor and composer, in rehearsal.

simply doesn't 'see' the orchestra at all, then the image of female conductors would appear to be quite crucial in terms of altering the public's perception of women and music.

Women in brass and military bands

It has been even more difficult for women to play in a band – especially a military band – than it has to play in an orchestra. This is partly because they have had to fight against old-fashioned ideas that they were too weak to play wind and brass, and that it would ruin their looks. Another reason is that bands have often been closely connected with military life or with heavy industries like mining and steel, in which women have traditionally not taken a great part.

Even so, there were all-women brass bands in the United States in the nineteenth century. As with orchestras, it was war – in this case the First World War (1914–18) – that gave women the first real chance to join civilian and marching bands. Unlike the orchestras, however, most bands went back to being all-male once the fighting was over.

Today, there are many mixed marching bands in the United States, like the University of Southern California and University of Kansas bands. In Britain, the number of women members of the National Brass Band Association has increased steadily over the years and the bands of the WRAC and WRAF are among the finest of their type.

Women are also gradually being accepted as conductors of such groups. One of the pioneers in this area is Avril Coleridge-Taylor, who has been one of the most distinguished conductors of the Royal Marines. She has also appeared with the BBC Symphony Orchestra and the London Symphony Orchestra.

Women in dance and jazz bands

Women encountered the same difficulties in dance and jazz bands. When they found that they could not get work in male groups, many women set up bands of their own. Two of the most famous were the International Sweethearts of Rhythm, and the Ivy Benson All-Girl Dance Band.

The International Sweethearts of Rhythm

The International Sweethearts of Rhythm was a multi-racial, all-women's jazz band which was set up in the 1940s. Under its conductor Ina Rae Hutton, it toured all over the United States, becoming so popular that, in several cities, mobs of people fought to get into its concerts. Several of the players, like the tenor saxophonist Vi Burnside, were amongst the greatest of the time, and Louis Armstrong and Count Basie, reckoned by many to be the 'kings of jazz', would stand in the wings listening to them. During the Second World War, they broadcast to American soldiers overseas and later, billed as the 'Greatest Girl Band in America', they toured Europe, giving concerts in France, Belgium and Germany. One of their first concerts was given at Germany's famous Nuremberg Opera House.

Not that their path was always smooth. Because of its black players, the band faced a lot of opposition in the American Deep South. After

Ivy Benson playing saxophone with her All-Girl Dance Band in 1945, the year of their triumphant European tour.

The Lydia D'Ustebyn Ladies' Swing Orchestra, showing baritone, alto and tenor saxophone, drums, congas, flugelhorn, trumpet, trombone, double bass and electric bass.

the war, when many of the players married and had families, it became difficult to recruit new members, and the group eventually had to fold up.

The Ivy Benson All-Girl Dance Band

Like the International Sweethearts of Rhythm, the Ivy Benson All-Girl Dance Band also had difficulties. At first they were not allowed into the ballrooms and were forced to play in tea-shops, where they had little status and even less money. Another problem was that, because they had not 'grown up' in jazz bands, not many of them had ever had the chance to learn to improvise – that is, make up the music as you go along, an essential skill in real jazz. So all the music – including the most complicated solos – had to be composed beforehand and written out note by note. Then it had to be rehearsed over and over again, so that all the players knew the music so

well that anyone listening would think that it was being made up on the spot.

The big break for Ivy Benson's band came during the Second World War when Mecca dance halls were forced to recruit women. From then on, they went from strength to strength and, like the International Sweethearts of Rhythm, they became very popular, especially with American troops based in Europe.

Women's bands since the Second World War

Since then, several all-women bands have appeared on the jazz and soul scene. Some of them, like Lydia D'Ustebyn's Ladies' Swing Orchestra, the Guest Stars and Hipscats, have not had a very long life, but they have been a very important training ground and outlet for many highly talented professional women musicians.

One of the largest of these bands was SOS, which had more than twenty players. This band was strong on improvisation. It also changed the sound of this kind of music by making all the instruments equal, rather than treating some as star (solo) instruments and others as just backing, as had usually been the case in the past. The same approach was taken up by Fig which, until it folded in 1981, built up quite a following in Europe and attracted much attention because of its attempts to break down the traditional barriers between jazz and rock.

Women in rock and pop

Women rock bands

One of the first real rock female bands was Fanny, which appeared in the United States in the early 1970s. This was followed by such groups as Isis, Birtha and Pride of Women. But it was when punk arrived a few years later that women really made a breakthrough into this kind of music, with line-ups like the Bloods, Snatch, the Slits,

The Bangles, whose successes in the charts belie the claim that all-female groups are not taken seriously.

and the Bodysnatchers. Later renamed Belle Stars, the last group reached third place in the British charts with 'Sign of the Times'.

Some have claimed that all-female pop and rock groups are no more than passing gimmicks, not to be taken seriously. However, more and more of them have appeared since the mid 1980s and their success in the charts shows that they are being taken seriously. Fuzzbox, with 'X X Sex' and 'Love in the Sky' for example, are a case in point. More significantly the Bangles have scored hits on both sides of the Atlantic with singles such as 'Manic Monday', 'A Hazy Shade of Winter' and the chart-topping 'Walk Like an Egyptian'. Their LPs 'Different Light' and 'Everything' have also been great successes. This group has been awarded gold and platinum discs and in 1987 won the coveted British Pop Industry's 'Best International Group' award.

The group generally regarded as the most successful female vocal group of the 1980s is Bananarama. Unlike many similar groups before them, they took control of their own careers at an early stage and projected an image of great strength and independence.

Forming an alliance with Fun Boy Three, they reached the Top Ten with 'Really Saying Something', with backing from the male trio. They went on to score further hits with 'Sky Boy', 'Na Na Hey Kiss Him Goodbye', 'Robert de Niro's Waiting' and 'Cruel Summer'. The last item was featured in the film *Karate Kid* and became their first American hit. Their first American No. 1 was the single 'Venus' which was also a Top Ten success in Britain. Further hits in the United States and Britain include 'I heard a Rumour', 'Love in the First Degree' and 'I want you Back'.

In 1987, Siobhan Fahey left the group to form Shakespeare's Sister which two years later made the charts with the single 'You're History' and the album 'Sacred Heart'.

As well as all-female line-ups we are also seeing more and more mixed groups where men are in the minority. One of these, Amazulu, in fact started as an all-woman reggae band. But when their drummer left, they decided to employ the best one they could find, who happened to be a man. And The Shop Assistants, who for several years were high in independent pop charts, before entering the charts proper, have three women to one man.

A reversal of roles is also being seen. For example, Fun Boy Three, the male trio, has on more than one occasion provided the vocals to the backing of female bands. This is in direct contrast to the usual pattern of women doing the singing, while men look after the instrumental side.

Even among women vocalists the styles are changing. Annie Lennox of the Eurythmics, one of the most dynamic rock bands of the 1980s, dresses and behaves on stage in a manner which has traditionally been more associated with male performers. Similarly Madonna, one of the most popular teenage idols of the 1980s, has created a whole new image for female singers with her assertive challenging of conventional attitudes in such hit singles as 'Papa Don't Preach' and 'Like a Prayer'.

Women guitarists

All these rock and pop groups, of course, have given women the chance to shine on those instruments which were for a long time 'reserved' for men. The bass guitar has undoubtedly proved the most attractive to women. For many years it was felt that the instrument was too heavy for women to play. One of the first to disprove this was the American session musician Carol Kaye. In the 1960s and early 1970s she provided the bass to dance records, television and film tracks, jazz and punk albums as well as to most of the well-known hit singles of the time – including those by Elvis.

She was followed in the 1970s by several other female bass guitarists in groups like the Slits, Mistakes, Au Pairs, Tour de Force, Talking Heads and Raincoats. Much of their music was influenced by reggae, in which the bass plays a very important part. So these women were really the driving forces of the groups.

Women guitarists have not just copied men's style of playing. Instead, they have brought a whole range of new approaches to the instrument. Carol Kaye, for example, abandoned finger-playing in favour of the plectrum and, in her hands, the bass guitar became almost another

Joan Armatrading, a solo performer and – like so many contemporary women artists – a highly successful singer–songwriter.

melody instrument rather than just a producer of dull, repetitive rhythms.

The same could be said of Vicki Aspinall of the Raincoats. Aspinall made a study of African pop music. There, instead of some instruments being lead, and others back-up, some melody and others bass, all the players are on an equal footing, with none of them just playing a supporting role. This idea certainly carried over into her style of playing.

Other women guitarists – Joan Armatrading is an example – have developed individual styles because they have taught themselves, while others, like Kim Clark, have adapted their style to suit the particular shape of their hands.

Some have changed not so much the style of playing as the style of presentation. Viv Albertine of the Slits, and Carol Colman of Kid Creole and the Coconuts, for example, have tried to move away from the classic rock musician's pose and experimented with sitting rather than standing.

Women drummers

A change of style can also be seen in women's approach to the drums. There are not nearly as many female drummers as guitarists. But, since the late 1970s, more and more have come on to the scene, not just in all-female groups but also in mixed groups such as the Communards, the Desperados and the Thompson Twins.

Traditionally, drummers have been restricted to just playing the rhythmic back-drop to the music, with a few breaks now and then to let the player show off. Several women have tried to move away from this to give the drums a central place in the music. Some have tried to treat them as melody instruments.

Since the early 1980s many women drummers

The Thompson Twins, showing their drummer Alannah Thompson.

have pared down or adapted their kits. Trudy Baptiste, who played with the London group King Trigger, used a kit made up entirely of snare drums, while Sandra Brown of Abandon Your Tutu hardly ever uses hi-hat cymbals or the bass drum pedal.

Others, in bands like Scritti Politti and Swann's Way, have brought in new instruments like congas and hand-held percussion. Not everybody approves of this: Alannah Currie, for example, has complained that people do not take her seriously when she plays instruments like marimbas, timbales and cowbells.

All this of course makes a mockery of the old-fashioned idea that women did not have the strength to be percussionists. Even if that were true, the argument would have been defeated by the microtechnological revolution with its touch-sensitive drum machines.

Some people are now trying to claim that women will not be able to make full use of the new technology because they are no good with electronics. However, they have proved themselves more than equal to men in this area. One of the first musicians ever to use the synthesizer was the 1960s singer and keyboard-player Annette Peacock, who was given one by the inventor Robert Moog. She has been followed by many others like Carrie Booth of the Monochrome Set and Thompson Twins, Pia of Phillip Boa and the Voodoo Club, and Gillian Gilbert of New Order. Gillian Gilbert produced some amazing synthesizer sounds on the hit single 'Blue Monday', which at the time was Britain's best-selling 12-inch disc ever.

'Twice as tough, twice as good?'

Everything you have read so far shows quite clearly that, if they are given the same opportunities as men, women can do just as well, in any branch of the performing world.

The same is true for composition. But here again, women have often had to fight hard to prove the point, as you will soon see.

You have to be twice as smart, twice as tough and twice as good as the men just to get to the bottom of the rank where you can eat and pay your rent.

Carol Colman, bass guitarist with Kid Creole and the Coconuts, 1983

There is the same pressure for everybody. It is just that for women it's made so much more of a big deal.

Alison Moyet, formerly vocalist of Yazoo, 1987

- **With which of these ideas do you agree most?**
- **Why?**

'Men compose symphonies, women compose babies'
TIME MAGAZINE, 10th January 1975

WOMEN *as* COMPOSERS

Write down the names of all the male composers you can think of. Now do the same for women composers and then compare the two lists. The second list will probably be far shorter than the first, and the same will probably happen if you try the same test on your friends and teachers.

Some people have tried to claim that this proves women are just not capable of composing.

All creative work is well known as being the exclusive work of men

wrote one German musician in the nineteenth century, and the American music critic, George Upton, had this to say at around the same time:

Woman will always be the recipient and interpreter but there is little hope that she will be the creator.

Even in this century, Sir Thomas Beecham argued that:

there are no great women composers, never have been and probably never will be.

But the fact is that women have been composing for thousands of years. The first woman composer in recorded history was the Egyptian Iti, who lived around 2450 BC. She was so famous that she appears in several writings and pictures of the time. One Egyptian nobleman was so impressed by her compositions that he had a relief of her carved on his tomb, in the hope that he would still be able to enjoy her music in the afterlife. As you will see, Iti was the first of a very long line stretching right up to the present day.

So why are these women composers not better known? There are several reasons for this.

Lack of experience

Although women have composed, few have written the kind of music which people like to think of as 'important'. When we talk about famous classical composers, these tend to be people who have written works for several different solo instruments or long, complicated works – like symphonies, concertos, overtures, operas and oratorios – for large orchestras and choirs. But composers can only do this under certain conditions.

To write for any instrument you need to know a lot about it. You need to know how high or low it can go and what kind of music sounds best on that instrument. It is no good, for instance, expecting a trumpet to play several long, high notes, because the performer would not have the lip or lung power to produce them. In the same way, trills are fairly easy to play

Si Hei Lwli 'Mabi

Traditional

English translation by Aelwyn Pugh

Hush my litt - le dar - ling, The ship is sett - ing sail

Hush my dar - ling ba - by, The cap - tain's at the rail.

Hush o hush my dar - ling sweet, Sleep my swee - test an - gel sleep,

Hush my litt - le dar - ling, The ship is sett - ing sail

Look at the words of this Welsh folk song.

- **For what occasion do you think this song was originally composed?**
- **Who do you think is more likely to have made it up – a man or a woman? What leads you to your conclusion?**
- **Try singing the song. If you have access to a guitar, add the chords to it or try arranging the chords for pitched percussion. Your teacher could help you with this.**
- **Try out different types of accompaniment until you find the one that sounds best. Which do you think is better, a solo performance or a group performance of the song? Why do you think that?**

on the piano but can be very difficult to sing. The best way to find out what various instruments can do is to play them. It is no accident that composers often write their finest music for the instruments which they have most experience of playing.

We have already seen that in the past, women were encouraged only to sing, or to play a small number of instruments. So when they came to compose, they had to confine themselves to songs, or to pieces for keyboard or harp. Since the type of instruments which they played were not usually part of large groups like orchestras, they found it particularly difficult to write works like symphonies and concertos.

Of course, it is not impossible for composers to write for instruments which they cannot play themselves. But to do that well, they need to work alongside people who are able to play them and who will try out various ideas to see whether or not they work. The composers in the best position to get such help are those who meet lots of performers – orchestral players, conductors, organists and so on. As we have seen, women were not usually in a position to do this.

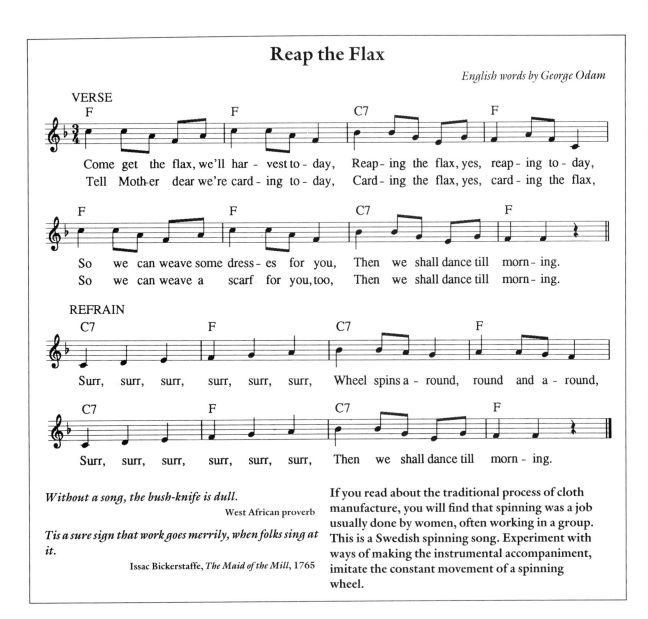

Reap the Flax

English words by George Odam

VERSE

Come get the flax, we'll har-vest to-day, Reap-ing the flax, yes, reap-ing to-day,
Tell Moth-er dear we're card-ing to-day, Card-ing the flax, yes, card-ing the flax,

So we can weave some dress-es for you, Then we shall dance till morn-ing.
So we can weave a scarf for you, too, Then we shall dance till morn-ing.

REFRAIN

Surr, surr, surr, surr, surr, surr, Wheel spins a-round, round and a-round,

Surr, surr, surr, surr, surr, surr, Then we shall dance till morn-ing.

Without a song, the bush-knife is dull.

West African proverb

Tis a sure sign that work goes merrily, when folks sing at it.

Issac Bickerstaffe, *The Maid of the Mill*, 1765

If you read about the traditional process of cloth manufacture, you will find that spinning was a job usually done by women, often working in a group. This is a Swedish spinning song. Experiment with ways of making the instrumental accompaniment, imitate the constant movement of a spinning wheel.

Lack of training

Another reason why women found it difficult to write large, complicated works was that they did not usually get the necessary training.

It is not very difficult to make up a short tune and fit a simple accompaniment underneath it. But it is far more difficult to write music for many different performers or to compose a work which goes on for a long time. To do that, you need a considerable amount of technical knowledge. Composers usually acquire this in two ways: by studying music at school, college or university, or by being directly involved in music-making, and getting on-the-job training in the process.

As you already know, for a long time women found it very difficult to get any kind of musical training. Even in the conservatoires of the nineteenth century, it was many years before women were allowed into the composition classes. As for on-the-job training, this was even more difficult because women were not encouraged to follow any career, let alone a musical one.

Lack of publicity and publishing opportunities

Even when women composers did produce large-scale works, they often found it very difficult to get publicity. To become well-known, composers need to have their works performed many times, in many different places. One way of doing this, which was used a great deal in the past, is for composers themselves to travel around putting on performances of their works in various towns and cities. For women, with their responsibilities for home and family, this was virtually impossible. There was also a feeling that it was not right for women to appear in public.

Another way to develop a reputation is to publish music. But again, many women composers found this difficult. As recently as 1931, for instance, the American composer Ruth Crawford Seeger was more or less told by the director of the Viennese publishing house, Universal Edition, that her works could not be considered because they were by a woman. About fifty years before that the English composer Ethel Smyth was told the same thing by the director of the Breitkopf and Hartel publishing company. Unlike Seeger, Smyth managed to get him to change his mind. 'But', she wrote, 'having listened to all he said about women composers . . . I asked for no fee! Did you ever hear of such a donkey!'

One way in which many women composers tried to avoid such problems was to publish their works under men's names. Fanny Hensel, for example, published several works under that of her brother Felix Mendelssohn. Exactly how many times she did this is unclear. We do know for certain that a duet described by one leading magazine as the best composition in Mendelssohn's Opus 8 collection was in fact by his sister. But the most interesting evidence comes from Mendelssohn's diary for 1842. That year he visited England and was invited to Buckingham Palace to play to Queen Victoria and Prince Albert. At one point, Mendelssohn invited the Queen to sing while he accompanied her. She chose a song called 'Schöner und Schöner' because it had been written by Felix – or so she thought. He tells us,

I was obliged to confess that Fanny had written the song (which I found very hard, but pride must have a fall).

Hensel was by no means the only one to do this. Clara Schumann often published under her husband Robert's name. The nineteenth-century composer Irene Baumgas used the name Victor René, while another composer of the time, Augusta Holmes, called herself Herman Zerta. Even in the twentieth century, the Dutch composer, Else Antonia van Epen de Groot, has published several works – especially film scores – under the name Derek Laren. These are just a few of the ones we know about. Over the centuries, there must have been many others who have not yet been identified, and possibly never will be.

The oral tradition

To build up a picture of how music has developed, historians have to rely a great deal on the music of the past which still exists in manuscripts or printed copies. These can only give an incomplete picture, because a tremendous amount of music has been lost or destroyed or has yet to be rediscovered. This is an even greater problem with the works of women composers.

A great deal of their music would have been composed for private performance and would never have been written down or, at best, only roughly scribbled on loose bits of paper.

Not that written copies are essential for music to survive. The folk music of the world is full of lullabies, songs of farewell to fathers as they go to sea, laments for fathers killed in battle, or songs to teach children to count, to name colours and so on. These, no doubt, were first made up by ordinary women as they went about their daily lives; women whose names will never be known to us.

It is quite obvious, then, that there is no question that women can compose. They have produced far more than we shall ever know about, often against the greatest odds. Because of their circumstances, many of them concentrated on limited areas of composition which, simply because of accidents of taste, have not always attracted much attention.

However, there are a number of women composers who have written large-scale works which are quite equal to those by men. We shall now turn our attention to some of these women.

Hildegard of Bingen (1098–1179)

We have already seen that, in the past, nuns were in a far better position than lay women to make music. This consisted mostly of hymns and chants and a lot of it was written by the nuns themselves. There is hardly a century when nuns have not produced important compositions. Unfortunately the names of the composers have not always come down to us and their works have often been lost. Luckily, in the case of one of the finest of the nun-composers, we know her name, and can still perform many of her works. She was Hildegard of Bingen, a German nun who lived in the twelfth century.

The tenth child of a noble family, she was sent to the convent at Disibodenburg at the age of eight where, amongst other things, she learnt to read music and to sing. She must have been one of the most able nuns in the convent because in 1136 she became its head. In 1147, she and her followers moved to Rupertsburg near Bingen in the Rhine Valley, where she stayed as abbess until she died.

She soon became famous as a teacher, poet and writer. She wrote several books on theology, science and medicine – her *Materia Medica* was one of the most important medical textbooks of the Middle Ages. She was also famous for her visions, in which she claimed to get messages straight from God. Because of this, some of the most important people of the day came to her for advice – including popes, emperors and kings.

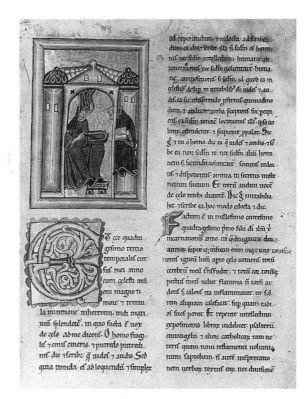

Hildegard of Bingen, the medieval composer, visionary, writer and musician, depicted in a twelfth-century manuscript as receiving a revelation from Heaven. She records this on a wax tablet with a stylus while a monk waits to make a parchment copy.

'The harp whose strings are plucked by God'

According to Hildegard, her music also came from heaven, and she described herself as a harp whose strings were plucked by God. To underline this, she called the collection of her compositions *Symphonia Armonie Celestium Revelationum* (Symphony of the Harmony of the Heavenly Revelations).

The book is made up of the songs which she composed between 1151 and 1158. Most of these were written in honour of saints like Mary, Ursula and Rupert and were no doubt meant to be sung by the nuns in her own convent, all of whom were trained singers.

She also wrote a book on the history of music, and a musical play called *Ordo Virtutum* (Play of the Virtues). This is very important, since it is the earliest known example of a Morality Play. In the days when most people were illiterate, the Church relied heavily on drama to teach the stories and messages of the Bible. This play by Hildegard tells of the battle between Evil and Good in the struggle to win control of the human soul.

So important a person was Hildegard that, after her death, there were several attempts to have her declared a saint. She was never actually given that title, but she does have a feast day which, in the Roman Catholic Church, is celebrated on 17th September.

On the next page is an extract from a piece by Hildegard, 'O Ignis Spiritus'.

O Ignis Spiritus

Hildegard of Bingen

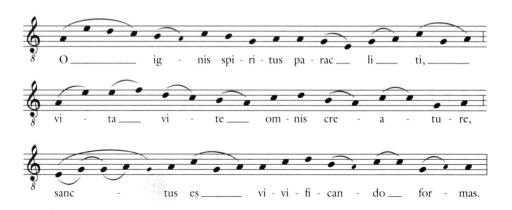

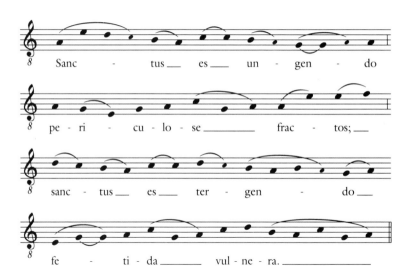

O ignis spiritus paracliti,
vita vite omnis creature,
sanctus es vivificando formas.

    Sanctus es ungendo
    periculose fractos;
    sanctus es tergendo
    fetida vulnera.

O fire of the comforting Spirit,
life of the life of all Creation,
you are holy in quickening all Kind.

    You are holy in anointing
    the dangerously stricken:
    you are holy in wiping
    the reeking wound.

This is an extract from a more extended plain chant than the one on page 11. Here again, when performing it, aim for a smoothly flowing sound, in which the rhythm of the words is reflected in the rhythm of the music. There are several of Hildegard's works available on recordings – see the *Listening list*.

Raffaella Aleotti (c. 1570–after 1646)

Ferrara, you will remember, became famous in the late sixteenth century because it had two very important music centres: the court of Duke Alfonso, and the convent of San Vito. Working in either of these would have been a wonderful experience for any musician, but Raffaella Aleotti was lucky enough to have the experience of both.

Raffaella Aleotti was the daughter of Gianbattista Aleotti, Duke Alfonso's personal architect and engineer. Growing up in that setting, Raffaella would have known some of the finest musicians of the day and would have heard the wonderful performances they produced. She must have shown a great deal of interest and talent because she was soon having harpsichord and composition lessons from some of them. But her real chance came when she entered the convent of San Vito.

Here there were several superb choirs and instrumental groups, and the training which the nuns were given was unequalled anywhere else. Raffaella proved to be an outstanding musician. In 1593 she became the conductor of the most important group, the *Concerto Grande*. This group was already well-known in Italy but, under Raffaella's direction, it reached even greater heights and was praised by many of the finest composers of the day.

In 1598, the *Concerto Grande* performed before the Pope and the Queen of Spain. The Queen was so impressed that she tried to persuade Raffaella to go back to Spain with her as her personal organist. But Raffaella preferred to stay in Ferrara where she could work with a number of very fine musicians.

'Sacrae Cantiones' and the polyphonic style

It was for these musicians that she wrote the *Sacrae Cantiones* (Sacred Songs). This was published in 1593 and is the only collection of her works known to have survived. It is very important because it is the first set of compositions by a woman ever to be written in what is known as the polyphonic style. This is a style of writing which involves large numbers of voices or instruments, all of which are given long complicated melodies to play, which have to be blended together to produce a complete sound.

It is by no means easy to write in the polyphonic style, and it requires a great deal of musical knowledge and training. For a long time it was felt that women could not and should not produce such music but should write only simple melodies with a few accompanying chords. In fact, on several occasions, popes, archbishops and bishops tried to forbid women from performing or writing in this style. Raffaella showed that women were more than capable of writing polyphonic music, so long as they had the right type of training.

Sacrae Cantiones is also very important for another reason. At this time, Italian composers were beginning to experiment with a new style of writing where groups of instruments and voices were set against each other in a kind of musical competition. This 'concertante style' was eventually to lead to the concertos of later centuries. It is interesting that *Sacrae Cantiones* contains some of the earliest examples of the concertante style ever produced.

Raffaella Aleotti was therefore a pioneer not just among women but among musicians in general.

Francesca Caccini (1587–c. 1640)

The trends set in Ferrara soon spread, and the first person to copy the idea of the *concerto di donne* outside that city was Giulio Caccini, chief composer at the court of the Medici family in Florence. Giulio frequently experimented with new ideas: he was, for example, one of the leading composers of opera which at that time was only just beginning to develop as a form of composition. His wife was a singer.

In 1587, Giulio's daughter Francesca was born, and from quite an early age showed that she had inherited her parents' gifts. Giulio took great pains to develop her talent, teaching her to read music and to sing, taking her to rehearsals and performances at court and introducing her to the many fine musicians in his choir and orchestra.

Aure Volante

Duet from Caccini's opera La Liberazione di Ruggiero
dall' Isola d'Alcina

**Try performing this duet. You will need
two singers and a keyboard player. The
accompaniment could also be played on three
pitched instruments, if you preferred.**

Francesca made her first public appearance as a singer when only thirteen at the wedding of Maria, a daughter of the Medici family, to the French King Henri IV. Like many noblewomen marrying into a foreign family, Maria wanted to keep in contact with her home even when she moved to a new country. She therefore invited the Caccini family to perform at the French court, where Francesca must have made a particularly good impression because the King wanted her to stay. But she was refused permission by the Medicis and so, in 1607, she became an official member of the Florentine court.

Francesca sang regularly in theatrical performances, church services and private gatherings at court as well as in concerts all over northern Italy. She quickly developed a fine reputation, and by 1623 she was earning more money than any other courtier, apart from the Duke's personal secretary.

'Universally well-known as a composer'

Long before this she had started on her composing career. Her first attempts were mainly songs. In this, she was not so very different from many other women singers of the time, who also composed songs. Francesca, however, went on to compose far larger works. As early as 1606, she produced three extensive court entertainments and two years later she set a series of dramatic works to music.

By 1612, she was composing religious music, no mean feat at a time when lay women were not encouraged to take part in church music, let alone compose it. She also wrote musical scenes for the comedies performed at carnival time.

It was during the carnival of 1615 that her ballet, *Ballo della Zigane*, was performed at Florence's famous Pitti Palace. In the following year, she made a highly successful visit to Rome, as part of the entourage of Cardinal Carlo di Medici who was anxious to impress his friends with the excellence of his family's musicians. It was to Carlo that she dedicated her *Primo Libro*, which was the largest collection of songs by any one composer, male or female, to have appeared in print at the time. This was followed by *Il*

Martirio di Sant' Agata (The Martyrdom of Saint Agatha), an early form of oratorio.

By 1624, Francesca was reported to be 'universally well-known as a composer'. But her most important work was still to come. This was the opera *La Liberazione di Ruggiero dall' Isola d'Alcina* (The Escape of Ruggiero from the Island of Alcina), performed in honour of the visit to Florence by the Polish prince Wladislaw Sigismund. It was not only the first full-scale opera to be written by a woman, but also the first by any composer to be based on a story other than Greek or Roman legend and history. It was performed in Warsaw in 1682, the first Italian opera ever to be heard outside Italy. This was an extremely important event because from then on the craze for Italian opera swept through Europe and was still the most important musical style in many countries well over a hundred years later.

After her death, in around 1640, many of Francesca's works were lost. But there can be little doubt that she was one of the most important composers – man or woman – ever to have lived.

Barbara Strozzi (1619–c. 1664)

Francesca Caccini was undoubtedly a great inspiration to the women composers who came after her. One of the most important of these was Barbara Strozzi.

Strozzi, like the two composers you have just read about, was lucky enough to be brought up in a very cultured musical home. Born in Venice in 1619, she was the adopted daughter of the poet and playwright Giulio Strozzi. Giulio was very closely involved in opera, writing the words (the libretto) for all the leading opera composers. In fact he wrote the libretto for the first Italian opera ever to be performed in Paris. He also knew all the important intellectuals of the day, through his membership of the Accademia degli Incogniti.

In Italy around this time there were several academies, or societies of learned people who met regularly to discuss current affairs, religion and philosophy, to demonstrate scientific inventions, and to listen to poetry, plays and music. In 1637, Giulio set up a new academy, the Accademia degli

A portrait of a female musician, recently identified as the composer Barbara Strozzi.
She is holding a viola da gamba, and a fragment of her music can be seen.

Unisoni, which met at his house. Barbara acted as the mistress of ceremonies at the meetings. One of her many duties was to perform songs for the entertainment of the members.

In this way Barbara came to know some of the most brilliant people in Italy, and she learnt a great deal from them. Giulio also arranged for her to be educated by private tutors and, most important of all, to study music with Francesco Cavalli, Venice's leading composer.

A modern composer

With all these advantages it is perhaps not surprising that Barbara became a very cultured woman and a famous singer. She also became well-known as a composer. Her first book of songs appeared in 1644. Its introduction makes it clear that she expects to be condemned for daring to publish music when she is only a woman. But she soon gained confidence and, between 1644 and 1664, she published eight books, containing over a hundred pieces. Most of these are arias for solo voice and keyboard and more extended works, known as cantatas.

Barbara published more cantatas than any other composer during the whole of the seventeenth century. Her compositions were also included in collections alongside works by the most outstanding composers of her time, thus demonstrating that her work was famous for its quality as much as for its quantity.

Unlike Francesca Caccini, Barbara Strozzi never held a post at court, nor did she have groups of performers on hand to perform her works, or rich patrons to commission them. Instead, she had to rely on her own initiative to write them and most of all to have them printed and published. It was mainly through her publications that she became well-known. In this way Barbara Strozzi was far closer to the modern idea of a composer (few modern composers have rich patrons with orchestras on hand to perform their works) than the other women we have looked at so far.

The composer Fanny Hensel. The sister of Felix Mendelssohn, it was made clear to her by her father that she could only exercise her musical gifts in the domestic sphere.

Fanny Hensel (1805–47)

The chance for girls to acquire both a general and a musical education improved tremendously in the nineteenth century. One girl who was able to take advantage of this was Fanny Mendelssohn. Born in Hamburg, Germany, in 1805, she studied both the piano and composition from a very early age. Like Barbara Strozzi before her, she had the advantage of living in a highly cultured home, where many of the finest musicians, writers, poets and artists of the day came to visit.

Sadly she was not encouraged to use the knowledge and training to make a career for herself. Her father discouraged her, warning her that, for her, music 'can and must only be an ornament', and he urged her to 'prepare more earnestly and eagerly for your real calling, the *only* calling for a young woman – I mean the state of a housewife'.

Things were very different for her brother Felix, who was always encouraged. So, while Felix was launched into a brilliant international career as a composer and conductor, Fanny had to be content to organise musical gatherings at the family estate in Berlin. But she made the very best of this and her gatherings soon became

famous for presenting first performances of some of the finest music of the time. Fanny often took part in these concerts, playing the piano and conducting a choir which she had formed.

A brother's jealousy?

Fanny also composed a large number of works. Precisely how many we shall never know, since she published many under her brother's name. But she certainly wrote over 200 solo songs as well as many piano works and several works for orchestra.

Women composers like the blind Maria Theresia von Paradis and Marianne Martinez had begun to produce orchestral works – including symphonies and concertos – in the eighteenth century. But it was still unusual for women to do this and it shows how advanced for her time Fanny was.

Her husband, the painter Wilhelm Hensel, was a great admirer of Fanny's compositions and tried to persuade her to publish them. Unfortunately, her brother was very much against her doing so. The result was that only two collections of her songs appeared in print during her lifetime, but not until 1847, the last year of her life. Two more collections appeared in 1850. But there are very many fine works by Fanny Hensel lying in libraries still waiting to be published. Until this happens, a full picture of a woman who was undoubtedly a very able and important composer cannot emerge.

Clara Schumann (1819–96)

You have already read about Clara Schumann the performer. As well as being one of the most brilliant pianists of the nineteenth century, she was also a composer.

She was taught composition as part of the excellent musical training which her father arranged for her, and she composed from early childhood right through to adult life. Her first composition, *Quatre Polonaises pour le Pianoforte* (Four Polonaises for the Piano), was published in 1831, when she was still only eleven. But probably the most famous work from her early years was the *Premier Concert*. This was a long, complicated work for piano and orchestra and was written to show off the soloist's brilliant technique. It was this, and other works of its type, which made such a name for Clara during her highly successful visit to Vienna in 1837. In a letter to her future husband, written on 21st December of that year, she tells him:

My second concert took place today and was another triumph. Of the many items in the programme my concerto had the best reception ... it has been well-received everywhere and has given satisfaction to connoisseurs and to the public in general.

At these concerts Clara would also improvise many elaborate works, thus giving further evidence of her abilities as a composer. In all, Clara published twenty-three sets of compositions. Many of them, of course, were for the piano, like the *Variationen über ein Thema von Robert Schumann* (Variations on a Theme by Robert Schumann) and *Drei Romanzen für Pianoforte* (Three Romances for Piano). She also wrote several works for piano and solo instruments, like the *Drei Romanzen für Pianoforte und Violine* (Three Romances for Piano and Violin).

Perhaps her most interesting compositions are her songs. She published at least three collections, but we cannot be sure of the extent of her output because, like many other women composers, she used a male pseudonym.

Clara obviously loved to compose. (See the next page for part of a piece she wrote when she was 19.) On one occasion she wrote:

There is nothing greater than the joy of composing something oneself, and then listening to it.

But she was also very uncertain about her talents, in spite of her obvious success, and one of her diary entries goes so far as to say:

A woman must not desire to compose – not one has been able to do it, and why should I expect to? It would be arrogance.

Andante con sentimento

componiert von Clara Wieck

An extract from a solo piece written by Clara when she was 19. If you are a pianist, try playing it, or ask a friend or teacher to do so.

The title emphasises the need to play the music with great feeling. Clara belonged to what is known as the Romantic movement in Western music. Notice the rich harmonies. These are produced by combinations of thick chords and the use of a wide range of notes close to each other on the keyboard.

Notice also the 'legato e dolce' at the beginning, emphasising the need to play the piece smoothly and sweetly, and the frequent use of rises and falls in volume. In bars 12 to 16, this is combined with the instruction 'to push the music forward'. (string. = stringendo, literally 'tightening')

gusted by the poor teaching. Instead she took up private lessons with a teacher who introduced her to other important composers such as Clara Schumann and Brahms.

Smyth produced many compositions during these student days, including a string quartet and sonatas for violin and piano, and for 'cello and piano. All these were performed in Germany. The first of her works to be heard in her native England was the Serenade for Orchestra which was performed at the Crystal Palace in 1890. This was soon followed by the overture *Anthony and Cleopatra*. George Bernard Shaw's review of the first performance gives some indication of how people still reacted to women composers:

When E.M. Smyth's heroically brassy overture to Anthony and Cleopatra *was finished and the composer called to the platform, it was observed with stupefaction that all that tremendous noise had been made by a lady.*

Ethel Smyth (1858–1944)

Unlike Clara Schumann, Ethel Smyth never had any doubts about her own ability to compose or about the talents of other women composers. This was probably just as well because, unlike Schumann, she had very little support from her family. Her father, a major-general in the British army, thought that music was immoral. So when Ethel first announced in 1876 that she wanted to got to the Leipzig Conservatoire to train to be a composer, he told her: 'I would sooner see you under the sod.'

But Smyth did not give up and, a year later, at the age of nineteen, she set off for Germany where she was immediately accepted into the composition class. This shows how rapidly the lot of women composers was improving. Less than twenty years earlier, the English singer and composer Clara Rogers had not been allowed to study composition. Smyth made several friends at the Conservatoire, including Grieg, Dvořák and Tchaikovsky who were all students there. But, after one year, she left the Conservatoire, dis-

Poster advertising Ethel Smyth's first successful opera, Der Wald.

The March of the Women

Ethel Smyth

Dedicated to the Women's Social and Political Union

1 Shout, shout, up with your song! Cry with the wind, for the dawn is break - ing;

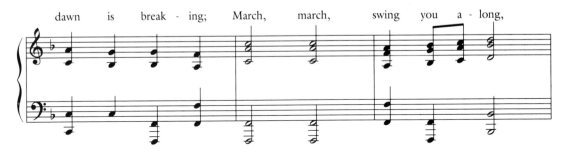

March, march, swing you a - long, Wide blows our ban - ner, and hope is wa - king.

Song with its sto - ry,

It has been claimed that Ethel Smyth once conducted a performance of 'March of the Women' with a toothbrush pushed through the bars of a prison window! While there is some doubt about the truth of this story, the song was certainly a great inspiration to women at the time.

Try to capture some of that spirit by giving your own rousing performance of the song.

2 Long, long – we in the past
    Cowered in dread from the light of heaven,
  Strong, strong – stand we at last,
    Fearless in faith and with sight new-given.
  Strength with its beauty, Life with its duty,
    (Hear the voice, oh hear and obey!)
  These, these – beckon us on!
    Open your eyes to the blaze of day.

3 Comrades – ye who have dared
    First in the battle to strive and sorrow!
  Scorned, spurned – nought have ye cared,
    Raising your eyes to a wider morrow.
  Ways that are weary, days that are dreary,
    Toil and pain by faith ye have borne;
  Hail, hail – victors ye stand,
    Wearing the wreath that the brave have worn!

4 Life, strife – these two are one,
    Naught can ye win but by faith and daring.
  On, on – that ye have done
    But for the work of to-day preparing.
  Firm in reliance, laugh a defiance,
    (Laugh in hope, for sure is the end)
  March, march – many as one,
    Shoulder to shoulder and friend to friend.

The first composition by Smyth to receive widespread praise was her Mass in D which was performed at the Royal Albert Hall in 1893. Sir Donald Tovey, one of the leading critics of the day, saw it as a high point in choral music, equal only to Beethoven's *Missa Solemnis*. One German conductor was so impressed by it that he told her that she should immediately 'sit down and write an opera'. And so, in 1898, Smyth started on the path which would bring her the greatest fame.

A composer of operas

Smyth's first opera *Fantasia* was written in German, and was not a great success. Her next opera *Der Wald* was far more successful. It was performed both in Berlin and London in 1902. Then, on 11th March 1903, it made history when it became the first opera by a woman ever to be performed at New York's Metropolitan Opera House. The audience were so impressed that they applauded the composer for over ten minutes.

Back in England, Smyth became more and more interested in the issue of votes for women, temporarily giving up her musical career in order to work for the cause. One of her songs, 'March of the Women', became a rallying cry for the suffragettes, who sang it on marches, at meetings, during riots and even in prison (see pages 48–49). Smyth herself spent two months in Holloway Prison in 1912, for smashing the windows of a cabinet minister's house.

She went back to full-time composing again in 1913 after a gap of two years, and produced *The Boatswain's Mate*, the first of her operas to be written in English. It had its *première* in 1916 and was soon to become a firm favourite with London audiences.

Around this time she began to go deaf. She produced two more operas, a Concerto for Violin, Horn and Orchestra, and a Symphony for Soprano, Bass-Baritone, Chorus and Orchestra, but eventually she was forced to abandon her composition work.

She immediately threw her energies into a new career, this time as a writer. From then on until her death in 1944, she produced ten books, all of which were instant successes. She also continued to write essays and articles calling for equal rights for women, and women musicians in particular.

Ethel Smyth refused to accept that being a woman should ever stop anyone from reaching the pinnacle of any profession. 'There is no sex in art,' she wrote. 'How you play the violin, paint or compose is what matters.'

Elizabeth Maconchy (b. 1907)

You might expect a composer of large-scale orchestral and choral works to have listened, from an early age, to vast amounts of music through broadcasts, records or live performances. Elizabeth Maconchy does not fit into such a pattern. She was born in Hertfordshire in March 1907 of Irish descent and spent her childhood in England and Ireland. Her family were not musical and she had no access to music on the radio or gramophone. Her only outlet was the piano.

When she entered the Royal College of Music, in 1923, as a sixteen-year-old student, she had only heard one symphony concert, one piano recital and one opera. However, she had been composing piano pieces since the age of six and, once at college, she soon established herself as a star of her generation. She won a scholarship to study in Prague and it was there, on her twenty-third birthday, that her Concertino for Orchestra was performed. Around this time, she entered for the Mendelssohn scholarship but narrowly failed to win it. Explaining the reason for this, one judge argued that if she had been given the prize she would 'only get married and never write another note'. She did get married, but neither this, nor raising a family, nor fighting a serious illness, stopped her composing.

In the 1930s publishers were still reluctant to publish anything by young women composers – apart from songs perhaps. Large-scale works were out of the question. Maconchy overcame this problem by sending a score of her orchestral work *The Land* directly to the conductor Sir Henry Wood, who decided to give it its first performance at the 1930 Promenade Concerts. It met with enthusiastic reviews: 'Girl Composer's Triumph, Masterly Work' ran the headlines in

Dame Elizabeth Maconchy, one of the leading British composers of the twentieth century.

Orchestras respectively, and *Profeta Mundi* (Prophet of the World) was produced for the Vienna Boys Choir in 1966.

Twenty years later, she wrote *Prayer Before Birth* for the Cantamus Girls Singers and it was with a performance of that work that they won the final of the Choir of the Year Competition.

Elisabeth Lutyens (1906–83)

Elisabeth Lutyens was the daughter of the famous architect Sir Edwin Lutyens. She studied in London and Paris before embarking on a career which led to the production of over 2000 published works. These include orchestral and choral music, chamber works, vocal music and instrumental music, film and radio scores and music for theatre, as well as three operas.

Musically speaking, she was one of the most radical composers of her generation. She was one of the first, for example, to introduce into Britain the technique of serialism, whereby the composer takes a *series* of notes and arranges them in a particular order, on which the melody and harmony of the piece then depend. Originally developed in Vienna by Arnold Schoenberg and others, this technique produced a radically different sound which drew much criticism from many sources.

Some of Lutyens' works in this style (such as her Chamber Concerto No. 1) aroused great animosity, and some, such as the chamber opera *Infidelio*, had to wait twenty years for their first performance. Her battles for acceptance, therefore, were about her style, not her sex – which is perhaps an indication of how much more seriously women composers have been taken in recent years.

one newspaper, which also described it as 'one of the best pieces of orchestral music written by any woman in recent years'.

From there, she went on to produce over a hundred published works, including her Symphony for Double String Orchestra and the dramatic monologue *Ariadne*. Her works have been performed widely in Britain, France Czechoslovakia, Poland and the USSR.

Between 1933 and 1984 she wrote thirteen works for the string quartet, one of her favourite areas of composition. She has also been active in the field of vocal music, producing a considerable amount of choral music and three one-act chamber operas: *The Sofa*, *The Departure* and *The Three Strangers*. For the last, she wrote her own libretto, based on a short story by Thomas Hardy.

Another of Maconchy's interests has been writing for children and for school and youth orchestras. 'Sinfonietta' and 'The Little Symphony' were written for the Essex and Norfolk Youth

Thea Musgrave (b. 1928)

Another composer who has made use of some of the most radical and exciting techniques of twentieth-century composition is the Scottish composer Thea Musgrave. Born in 1928, she studied at Edinburgh and Paris and became an influential force in British musical circles before moving to the United States where she now lives.

Musgrave has always been interested in the drama of music. One of the most dramatic situations, she finds, is the way in which, in a concerto, a soloist or small group is pitted against the force of a full orchestra. This can be seen in the following extracts from her choral setting of Dunbar's *Rorate Coeli*. Here singers are divided into a group of five soloists (*soli*) and a full choir (*tutti*). At times, the two groups are combined to produce a full, broad sound. At others, the soloists echo the main chorus or provide melodic, rhythmic or dynamic contrasts to them. As with so many twentieth-century works, there are frequent and sudden changes in volume from one bar to the next, and the composer makes considerable use of stark dissonances. You can see this in last full 'coeli' in the first extract, where all the notes are clustered together, and again in the second extract where pairs of voices (tenors and basses or the two alto parts) sing chords where each note is only a note away from the next one. All this highlights the drama of the text and the striving of the participants in the musical competition. This idea is taken even further in Musgrave's Viola Concerto. Each player is given music that is sharply defined, so that they can develop their own features and characteristics rather like characters in a play.

From this idea, she has developed what she calls 'space music'. Here soloists do not stand in one place during a performance, but move round the stage in order to highlight the nature and extent of their relationship with groups or individuals from the main orchestra. The use of space music is particularly evident in the Clarinet and Horn Concertos.

Given this interest in drama in music, it is hardly surprising that Musgrave should have turned to writing operas. Amongst her large-scale operatic works are *The Voice of Ariadne*, *Mary Queen of Scots*, *A Christmas Carol* and *Harriet, the Woman Called Moses*.

In 1981, she wrote an opera for radio, *An Occurrence at Owl Creek Bridge*. This involves a baritone, an actress, two actors and an orchestra performing with and against an almost continuous tape of sounds from the natural world. Thea Musgrave often uses taped sounds in her work, for example, in 'The Golden Echo I' for solo horn and tape, 'From One to Another I' for viola and tape, and 'Narcissus 1987' for solo flute with digital delay.

Musgrave is one of the most widely performed composers of her generation. Her works have been played by major orchestras in Britain, Europe and the United States, often conducted by Musgrave herself.

Rorate Coeli

Thea Musgrave

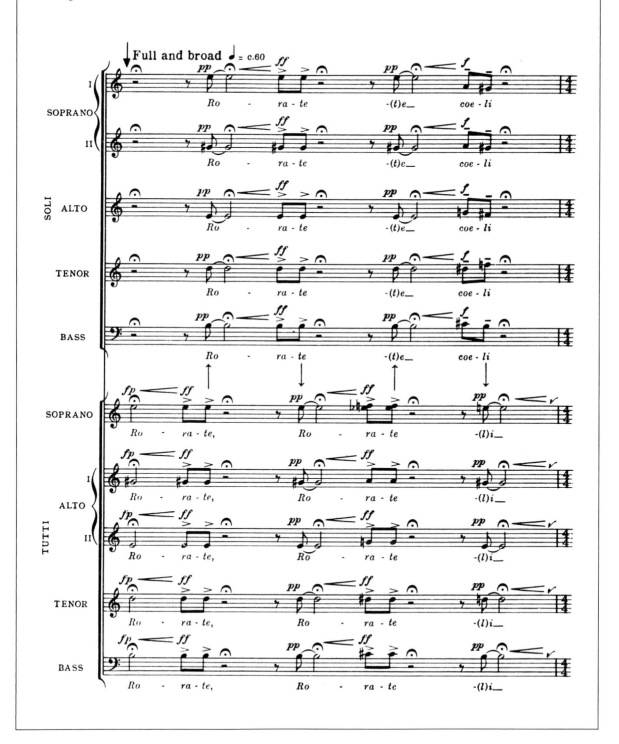

Nicola LeFanu, photographed the year she composed 'The Same Day Dawns'.

Nicola LeFanu (b. 1947)

Like Thea Musgrave, Nicola LeFanu, the daughter of Elizabeth Maconchy, is also fascinated by the dramatic aspects of music.

LeFanu read music at Oxford before studying for a year at the Royal College of Music in London. She was awarded first prize in 1970 for her Oboe Quartet, and also won (in 1972) a Gulbenkian Dance Award which enabled her to work with the Ballet Rambert, and (in 1973) the Mendelssohn Scholarship and a Harkness Award (the latter enabling her to study in the United States for a year).

One of the most interesting works resulting from her collaboration with the Ballet Rambert is *Anti-world* (1972), which is scored for actors and dancers as well as for singers. A solo male dancer controls the music and is in turn controlled by a singer or members of a small ensemble, each of whom behaves according to an established character.

This interest in combining art forms is also seen in LeFanu's chamber opera *Dawnpath* (1977). For this she provided not only the libretto and music but also a detailed choreographic plan. The work is based on two North American Indian myths. The first is the story of how the whole of creation arises from a single song. The second tells of how the first woman and first man on earth were given the choice of living for ever in darkness or dying, so that they could experience daylight as well as night. The opera has a cast of seven singers, five instrumentalists and a dancer who acts out the myth, becoming a tree, man's shadow, a deer or a representation of the process of growing.

Another major work by this composer is *The Same Day Dawns* (1977) for soprano, flute, clarinet, percussion, violin and 'cello. Like many other twentieth-century composers, LeFanu has turned to Eastern sources, drawing the words of this piece from Tamil, Chinese and Japanese poems.

The treatment of the words is typically twentieth-century. In the extract below, for example (pages 56–57), she exploits the emotional range of the voice by making use of a wide range of techniques, including speech and pitched speech, as well as conventional singing. She also makes use of the extremes of an instrument's range – for example the high 'cello notes – and relies on very light scoring, often using no more than one or two instruments at a time.

Another feature that makes this a typically twentieth-century work is the freedom given to the instrumentalists. At several points, LeFanu presents a series of short musical ideas, sets a time limit and then invites a particular group of performers to improvise freely within a loose framework indicated by the commentary. Where the music is more strictly scored, it often makes use of a wide range of time signatures in close succession (5/8 6/8 4/8 and 1/16, for example) rather than relying on one time signature for a considerable period, or for the full length of a piece.

The use of mixed time signatures can also be seen in the extract from LeFanu's *Chiaroscuro for Piano* (1972). The term 'chiaroscuro' is used in visual art to describe the contrasts of light and shade within a painting. Through a series of movements, LeFanu tries to bring out the light and shades of piano sounds.

Unlike the Romantic music of Clara Schumann, this piece is to be played unemotionally, without the pedal. When contrasting loud and soft sounds are used, they often appear suddenly, without the crescendo and diminuendo indications found in Schumann's music.

A particularly interesting feature of this extract is the way in which the melodic line is constructed. In bars 1 to 7, all 12 notes of the piano are presented in a specific order. From this 'row' of notes, the composer then builds further sections of the music. Thus in bars 7 to 12, the notes appear in basically the same order but with different rhythms, or at an octave higher or lower than their original pitch. In bar 13, the row is moved down so that it starts on Ab rather than D, but the basic relationships between the notes stay roughly the same. At bar 28, the melody of the right hand begins to be 'mirrored' by the left hand. Thus, when the right hand moves up the left hand moves down by the same distance, and so on. This approach to composition is known as *serialism*, which is mentioned above, in the section on Elisabeth Lutyens. The use of this technique puts LeFanu clearly in the mainstream of twentieth-century music.

The Same Day Dawns — Nicola LeFanu

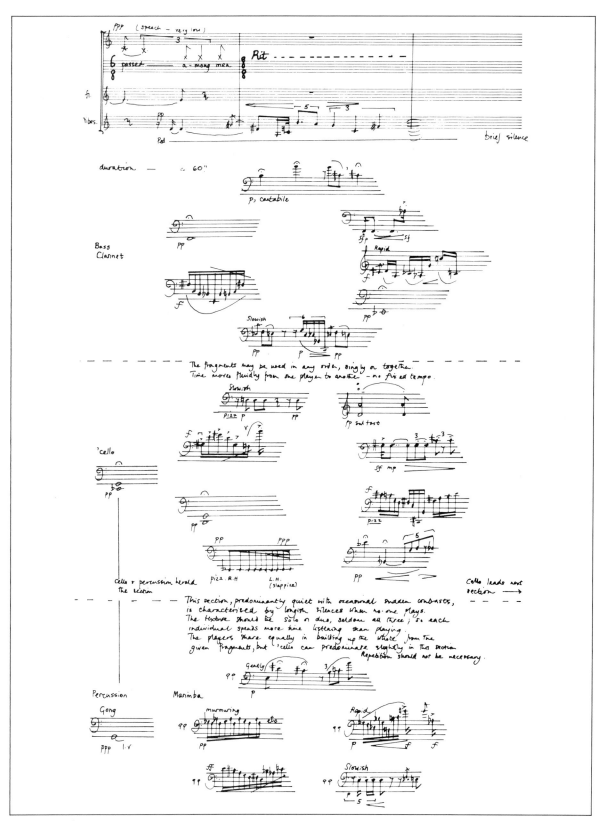

Chiaroscuro for Piano

(V.S.)

Judith Weir (b. 1954)

Judith Weir was born in Aberdeenshire and educated in London, where she studied composition with John Taverner.

Interest in myth and folklore lies at the heart of Judith Weir's music. Chinese culture, for example, has been the inspiration for such works as her music drama *The Consolations of Scholarship* and *A Night at the Chinese Opera*. Interest in Serbian and Spanish traditions has led to works like *Songs from the Exotic, A Serbian Cabaret, Romance of Count Arnaldos* and *Missa del Cid*.

She has also drawn considerably on medieval texts as in *King Harald's Saga*, which is based on an Icelandic saga. More recently, a commission to write *The Vanishing Bridegroom* for Scottish Opera has led to an exploration of Gaelic legends. As well as dramatic music, Weir has written a considerable number of instrumental works. Performers have often commented on how well suited her music is to their own technique and to the capabilities of specific instruments.

Judith Weir is now an established composer. Remember her name – you might like to make a special point of following her career.

C𝑜DA

One of the most exciting developments of the twentieth century has been electronic music. Many women have been active in this medium, particularly in the United States. It was estimated recently that there are about forty women actively studying electronic music in American universities: examples are Peg Ahrens, recording engineer at Kent State University, and Jean Eichelberger Ivey who set up the Peabody Conservatoire in Baltimore. Several other women have also helped to set up facilities for the study of electronic music.

The German composer Dolores Mertens will certainly go down in musical history because her song 'Moon Mission' was the first piece of music ever to be heard on the moon, when it was transmitted to the first astronaut to land there.

However, it is perhaps sobering to note that composer Beverly Grigsby publishes her works under the male pseudonym of Robert Russell Bennett. Could it be that although women composers are now composing for all media, publishing and conducting their works, and winning critical acclaim, they still face difficulties just because of their sex?

This book has given you no more than a brief history of women musicians, past and present. Now try to find out more about those discussed here, or try to discover the names of others. Next time you buy a record, look to see whether any women have been involved in writing, performing or producing it. Do the same when you watch a music programme on television, or go to a cinema or theatre when music is a feature.

If you are a girl with a lot of musical talent, consider whether you might not like to become a professional musician. Write to music colleges, read careers pamphlets, talk to people in the business to see exactly how you go about it: what training, qualifications and experience you need. Remember that every branch of the profession is open to you. If you have interest, ability and determination, there is no reason why you should not also become one of the ever-growing band of Women in Music.

LISTENING LIST

12th century

Hildegard of Bingen (1098–1179) Germany
  Hymns and Sequences (HYPE) CDA 66039
  Ordo Virtutum – morality play (DHM) (GD7705)

17th century

Caccini, Francesca (1587–c.1640) Italy
  'O che nuovo stupor' – madrigal (pub. 1618)
  (L'OL) 417 260–20H

18th century

Jadin, Hyacinthe (1769–1800) France
  Music for Wind Orchestra (ERAT) 2292–45005–2

Paradis, Maria Theresia von (1759–1824) Austria
  Sicilienne in E flat major (ASV) CDQ S6034

19th century

Hensel, Fanny (1805–47) Germany
  Piano Trio in G minor, Op. 11 (? 1847)
  (HYPE) CDA 66331
  Das Jahr – 12 Charakterstücke (1841)
  (CPO) CPO 999 013–2
  Vier Lieder ohne Worte – piano, Op. 6
  (CPO) CPO 999 015–2
  Gartenlieder, Op. 3 (1846) (BAYE) BR 100041
  Oratorium nach Bildern der Bibel
  (CPO) CPO 999 09–2

Lehmann, Liza (1862–1918) England
  'The swing-song' (CHAN) CHAN 8722
  'There are fairies at the bottom of our garden' –
  song (HYPE) CDA 66289

Schumann, Clara (1819–96) Germany
  Trio in G minor (before 1846) (HYPE) CDA 66331
  Three Romances – violin and piano, Op. 22 (1853)
  (CALL) CAL 9211
  Three Partsongs – unaccompanied choir (1848)
  (BAYE) BR1000 41

20th century

Beach, Amy Marcy (née Cheney) (1867–1944) USA
  Three Compositions – violin and piano, Op. 40
  (1898) (NORT) NR 9004–CD
  'Lento Espressivo' – violin and piano (1920s)
  (NORT) NR 9004–CD
  Romance – violin and piano, Op. 23 (1893)
  (NORT) NR 9004–CD
  Ballad – piano, Op. 6 (1894) (ARGO) 430 330–2ZH
  'By the still waters' – piano (1932)
  (NORT) NR 9004–CD
  'From grandmother's garden' – piano, Op. 97
  (1922) NR 9004–CD
  'A humming bird' – piano (1932)
  (NORT) NR 9004–CD
  Four Sketches – piano, Op. 15 (1892)
  (ARGO) 430 330–2ZH

Berberian, Cathy (1925–83) USA
  Stripsody (1966) (VIRG) VC7 90704–1

Boulanger, Lili (1893–1918) France
  'Attente' – mélodie (1911) (BAYE) BR 100041
  'Dans l'Immense' – mélodie (1916)
  (BAYE) BR 100041
  'Hymne au Soleil' – contralto, choir and piano
  (1912) BR 10041
  'Les Sirènes' – soprano, choir and piano (1911)
  BR 100041
  'Soir sur la Paine' – soprano, tenor, choir and piano
  (1913) BR 10041

Boulanger, Nadia (1887–1979) France
  Deux Pièces – 'cello and piano (1915)
  (NORT) NR 238–CD

Chaminade, Cécile (Louise Stéphanie) (1857–1944)
France
  Concertino for Flute and Orchestra, Op. 107
  (1902) (RCA) GK 85448
  'Automne' – piano, Op. 35 (CFP) TC–CF P4514
                             (KING) KCLCD 2002
                             (EMI) CD Z7 62523–2
  Sérénade Espagnole – piano (DECC) 417 289 – 2DH

Diemer, Emma Lou (b. 1927) USA
'Joy to the World' – organ   (VIRG) VC7 91088–2

Dring, Madeleine (1923–77) England
Four Betjeman songs (1976)   (HYPE) CDA 66289
'Mélisande, the far away princess and other songs'
(MERI) E77050

Giteck, Janice (b. 1946) USA
Breathing Songs from a Turning Sky – flute, clarinet,
bassoon, 'cello, piano, percussion and lights (1980)
(MODE) MODE 14
Callin' Home Coyote – burlesque – tenor, steel drums
and double bass (1978)   (MODE) MODE 14
*Thunder like a White Bear Dancing, ritual based on the
Mide Picture Songs of the Ojibwa Indian* – soprano,
flute, piano, percussion, slide projector (1977)
(MODE) MODE 14

Harrison, May (1891–1959) England
'The May song'   (SYMP) 1075

Hopkins, Sarah (b. 1958) Australia
Cello Cui – 'cello and 'cellist's voice (1986)
(NALB) NA028
Songs of the Wind – whirly   (NALB) NA 028

Lutyens, Elisabeth (1906–83) England
O Absalom – oboe quartet, Op. 122 (1977)
(BBC) BBC–CD 635
Encore – Maybe – piano (1982)   (LIBR) LRS 152
Stevie Smith Songs – song collection (1948–53)
(UNIC) DKPCD 9093

Maconchy, Elizabeth (b. 1907) England
String Quartets Nos. 1–4   (UNIC) DKPC 9080
String Quartets Nos. 5–8   (UNIC) DKPC 9081

Mahler, Anna (1879–1964) Austria
Lieder (1910, 1915, 1924)   (CPO) CPO 999 018–2
(OPUS) 9352 1887

Musgrave, Thea (b. 1928) Scotland
Impromptu No. 1 for Flute and Oboe (1967)
(BBC) BBC–CD 635
Four Madrigals – chorus a capella (1953)
(LEON) LE 328
Rorate Coeli – chorus (1973)   (LIBR) LRS 150
Verses of Love – chorus (1970)   (LIBR) LRS 150

Oliveros, Pauline (b. 1932) USA
'Bye Bye Butterfly'
1750 ARCH STREET RECORDS 1765

Roston, Elizabeth (1905–87) England
'Jesus Christ the Apple Tree' – carol
(ABBE) CDMVP827
(DECC) 425 500–2DM

Smyth, Ethel (1858–1944) England
Mass in D   (VIRGIN) VC7 91188–2
The Boatswain's Mate – opera (1916 – London)
(OPER) (2) OV 101/2
The Wreckers – opera (overture) (1906 – Leipzig)
(EMI) CDM7 69206–2

Van de Vate (b. 1930) USA
Chernobyl – orchestra (1987)   (CONI) CDCF 168
Concerto for Violin and Orchestra No. 1 (1986)
(CONI) CDCF 168
Concert Piece – 'cello and small orchestra (1985)
(CONI) CDCF 147
Distant Worlds – violin and orchestra
(CONI) CDCF 147

Weir, Judith (b. 1954) Scotland
Scotch Minstrelsey – songs   (ABCD) ABA 109–2

Williams, Grace (1906–77) Wales
Penillion for Orchestra (1955)   (ORIEL) ORM 1001
Ave Maris Stella – chorus (1973)   (CHAN) ABTD 1116
Mariners' Song – chorus, two horns and harp (1975)
(CHAN) ABTD 1116

Zaimont, Judith Lang (b. 1945) USA
Parable – A Tale of Abram and Isaac – soprano,
tenor, baritone, narrator, double chorus and organ
(1988)   (LEON) LE 328
'Serenade – To Music' – chorus a capella
(1981)   (LEON) LE 328